RECORD OF WRECKAGE

record of wreckage

---

musings of a melodramatic

ERICKA GARRAFFA

Ericka Garraffa

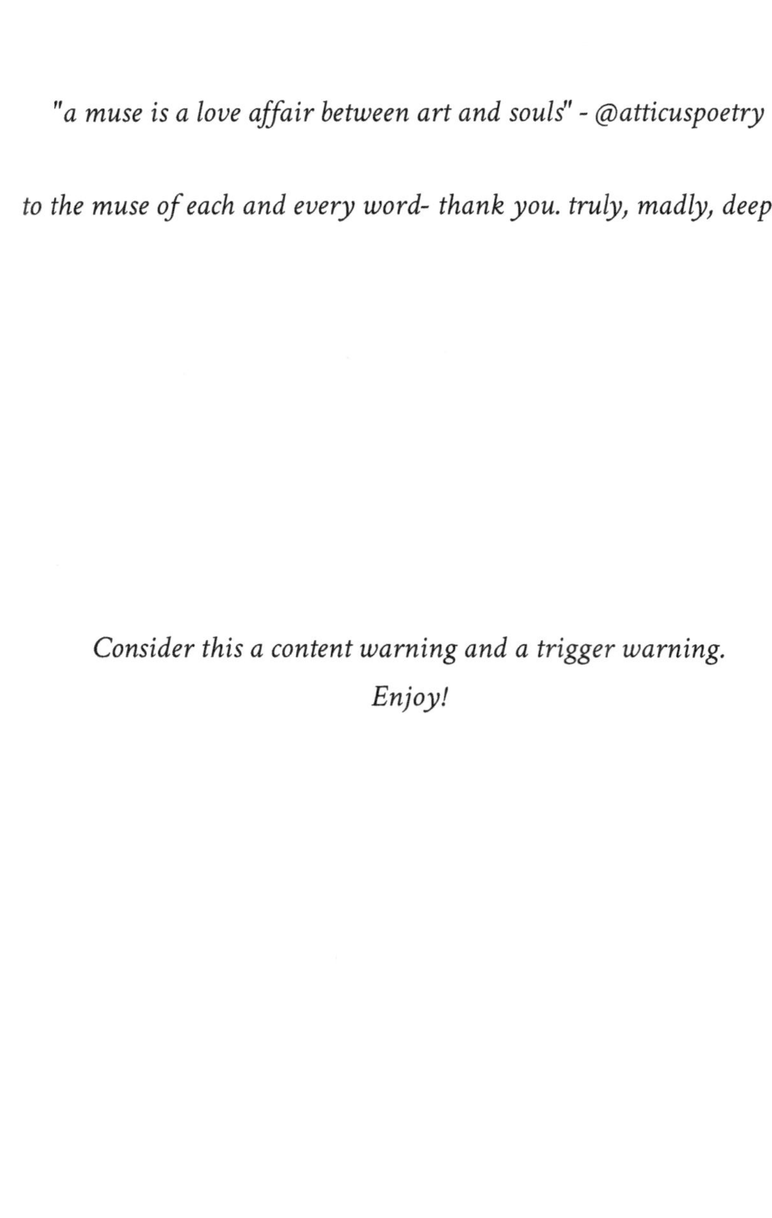

"a muse is a love affair between art and souls" - @atticuspoetry

to the muse of each and every word- thank you. truly, madly, deeply.

Consider this a content warning and a trigger warning.

Enjoy!

Trying to figure out how to keep the fire burning
without feeling like I'm suffocating it
but between soft lips is where I go to die
and it's goddamn when we touch
and I need you to teach me how to be enough
without being too much

-yours

I often let my intrusive thoughts linger
I allowed you to build a home inside my head from the moment we
met
and I wonder, now, if your name has any meaning behind it
an intrusive thought I can't help but laugh at
because of course it does
it means admirable and wonderful in Latin
and no wonder I spend so much time writing about you
even Shakespeare took his time playwriting for you
And it makes sense that the sky always makes me think of you
because even our solar system named a moon for you;
someone in Idaho said it means to be wondered at
and someone in the United Kingdom said it means worthy of
admiration
and I can't say I disagree
but they left some meanings out
your name means warm
and it means strong
even when you're scared
even when you're hurting
it means soft, it means to be cherished
it means healthy boundaries and it means self-love
your name means god and goddess
witch and wizard
it means not only a moon
but the sun and the stars
and the clouds and the rain
it means happy
dream come true

your name
your name means friend
your name means stranger
your name means I will always be waiting to hear you say my name
again
it means I will always be hoping to taste its sweetness on my lips
again
for now your name means stranger
it means one that got away
it means the door is always open when it's your name knocking
and I only dream of your name meaning love
hoping one day your name will mean friend again

-your name here

I love you.
Of course I love you, and you love me too
This I know.
But don't say you are in love with me
Until you understand what this means to me.
If you have reasons to love me,
Then don't love me.
"I love you because..." makes love conditional
And gives it an expiration date.
Love is wonderful, no matter what
But I don't want to give you reasons to love me.
Simply because I am wild and ever-changing,
Wandering, growing, evolving.
And once that reason changes,
So does your love for me.
I want a love that is just as unconditional and wild as I am.
Free and flowing like the rivers.
Just as bright and beautiful as the sun and moon and all the stars.
Sure,
I'd love to hear you ramble off a laundry list of things about myself
That you find worthy of your love.
But what about when the clouds roll in
And cover up the sunshine
And all I am is roaring thunder
And pouring rain
And lightning bolts ready to strike at any moment?
What then?
Does the love change, does it go away or lessen?
What kind of love is that?

More importantly,
Who wants a love like that?
I know I don't,
And I hope you don't ever settle for something so inferior.
You deserve unconditionally wild love,
As do I,
And I won't stop until I have it.
A love that sets my soul on fire
With a constant wind
That keeps it ablaze for eternity.

-unconditionally wild

I want to let it hurt
I want to open the floodgates until I am a river run dry
I want to be sad
But instead I'm thankful
I am thankful for the times we shared
I am thankful that I got to be a chapter or two
And even if I'm not your happy ending
I'm happy that your story continues
I am grateful that you let me hold parts of your life that most will
never touch
I am grateful for a glimpse of what we could have been
I am grateful to still have the pleasure of cheering you on from the
sidelines in every new endeavor
I am happy that I can be a part of your journey
And watch you grow into everything you deserve
And most of all
I'm grateful that there was time and space for me to take up
And I hope that there will always be some space left for me
I am happy that you are happy again.

-thank you card

You are god and goddess
The holiest of hells
Oh fucks and goddamns blooming in my mouth as the highest
praise
I want to leave an offering in your darkest depths
You wear your chaos like a crown
And I'm always on my knees for you
Let me worship you with my hands
My heart
My mouth
You are the ache unnamed
The ache untamed
Your body as the temple
Your laughter as the hymns
And I'm visiting this sacred place daily
Praying for a little bit of grace
Be easy on me Sunday
I am yet to confess

-take me to church

Remember me.
I hope you remember me.
I hope that you remember me softly
I hope that it never hurts to remember me
I hope you remember me as someone who loved you in the only
way I knew how to
And not that it always felt like being smothered
I hope you remember that I only ever wanted to see you smile
I hope you remember the time spent laughing together
And not the time spent crying apart
I hope you remember me as a light
As a star in the night sky
As a wildflower blooming from a crack in the sidewalk
I hope you remember me as a warm spring day
A butterfly or even a honeybee
I just hope that you remember me, and I hope it never pains you to
do so
Because I will always remember you
And even when it hurts
I hope I remember that holding you for a short time
was worth the memory that crawls in this empty bed with me now
I hope you remember me.

-remember me

To think that sweaters are made entirely of knots,
But the knots in my stomach when I saw you with her were not
good enough for sweaters.
Instead,
They made me want to burn every stitch of my clothing
That you have ever touched.

-relighting old flames

I want to slow dance with you when the lights go out in the middle
of a storm
We are merged in thought and bound by passion
And if this is a sin
Then reserve two thrones in hell for a god and their goddess
I'm having quiet conversations with flowers
And dancing on the edge of what this is and I don't care if I fall
Because you're such a pretty little poison to have in my veins
And I'm just a hurricane dressed as a girl
And it's fucked up there way you slip my spine around your finger
like a promise and make me want to keep it
Can you see the goddamn in my eyes when I look at you?
My words as fingers
And your fingers slipping over me
Your name slipping out of me
You are my cup of coffee
And I'm filling my cup with desires
Watching you settle into your divinity, as you become my favorite
oblivion
And I never know what I'm trying to say
But somehow my words always end up walking your way
Like I'm leaving trails of paper flowers for you to find me
Because I found god in the way you look at me when you're just
waking up
And the way your light is the only one that has ever been bright
enough to break through the fog in my head
Tell me all of your wildest dreams so that I have something to
aspire to be
-reckless abandon

As I sit here in this bed
Looking around the room
Everything seems normal
Almost everything
There's just one thing missing
And that one thing changes everything
Without you this house is not a home
I see empty walls and bare rooms
There is no one inside this castle of loneliness
Except the loneliest of them all
I feel unwelcome in this room we share
When you're not here sharing it with me
I can't sleep
Not without you
When you're laying next to me this bed is warm
Cozy
It has just enough room for the both of us
But tonight this bed is lonely, empty and cold
And I feel as if I could lie down and roll across it for light years
without the one I love sharing it with me
It seems endless
And this night without you does too
I want you home
I want you in our bed
I want you in my arms
This is where you belong
Where I belong
Where we belong
Together

Come back
Come home
This heart is not a home without the one who sheds a light in the
middle of all your darkness
Come back here
Be my light again

-prayers for sunshine in an empty cathedral

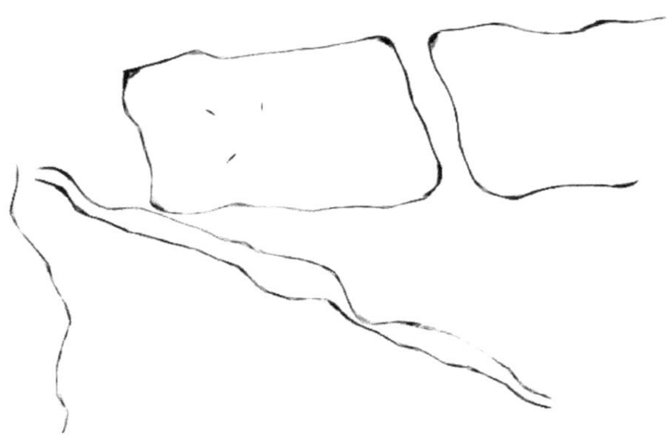

Pretending you're a stranger is the hardest thing I've ever done.
Pretending I don't want to reach out as I walk by
And brush against your skin.
Instead I keep my eyes fixed anywhere but your direction
In hopes that you won't see the longing inside of me.
Pretending I don't want to slide in that empty seat next to you and
talk about every little nothing.
Instead I'm laughing with my friends at a full table
and pretending your presence isn't so heavy I can feel it in my
chest.
Pretending I wouldn't be happy just catching you looking at me.
Instead I'm whispering sorrys for getting too close.
Pretending I don't know who you are is the hardest thing I've ever
tried to do.

-play pretend

Aesthetics on the playground.
Mine on the swings,
high-low-high-low,
the ups and downs.
Yours, running freely across the ground.
Always constant,
never slowing,
fearless.
I want you to love me but you always said consistency is key.

And I think
The hardest part of all
Is sitting with the stupid little feeling I get
When I remember
You love like moonlight
And I love like rain.
I love like heavy
I love like consuming
I love like falling
And you're the ground waiting to catch me.
And you,
You love in phases
But it's always so beautiful.

-phases

Love is about freedom
Love is about freedom
Love is about freedom
Love is about freedom
Love is about freedom
LET HER GO

-pep talk

Today.
Today my chest caved in.
Today my heart was shattered into a million unrecognizable pieces.
Today I lost it all.
Today everything I've come to know, everything I've come to love
Has been ripped from my hands.
I thought my grip was stronger.
I thought my grasping with both hands until my knuckles were
taut and white was enough to hold you here.
Today I learned I was wrong.
Today I heard you tell me you love me.
Today that turned out to be a different story.
Yesterday.
Yesterday I was holding you in my arms.
Yesterday you were my best friend.
Yesterday you loved me and I thought you meant it.
Yesterday I was whole.
Yesterday we were one.
Yesterday I had everything I ever needed and wanted right here
next to me
Yesterday you were mine.
Tomorrow.
Tomorrow I will still be broken.
Tomorrow I will still be empty and despondent.
Tomorrow you will be happy.
Tomorrow you will be fine.
Tomorrow I will still love you just as much as I did yesterday.
Tomorrow I will still hold onto hope.
Tomorrow I will pray for your love to return to me once again.

Tomorrow I will cry.
Tomorrow, when you walk out the door, I will feel the pain of
losing you all over again.
Tomorrow...
Tomorrow the sun will come out.
But it won't shine for me.

-Past. Present. Future.

I think my intuition always knew I'd never be able to keep you
it was a visceral feeling
like watching the sky darken
and the wind picking up
knowing that the storm was coming
and it was coming hell or high water
and I think I tried a little too hard to outsmart what fate had already decided
Like watching your favorite movie over and over
but still hoping for a different ending
and I think that's part of the reason I tried to hold you so tight
each time I had the chance to hold some part of you
and I think that some part of me will always hold space for you
you'll always be my moth but I think you prefer other flames
and I think
even if you never find your way back to this light
even in the rain
even through the dark
even when you're watching your favorite movie alone
I think but I will always be thinking about you

-overthinking

I catch your gaze
And you pretend you don't know me
And I play along
To keep my place in this stupid fucking game
But you can't pretend you don't know what my lips taste like from
past lives
And I can't pretend that I'm not wishing I didn't see her running
her fingers along your arms like a roadmap
But I'm a sore loser
And I'm hoping that map leads you back here to me

-other destinations

I pick up a pen and somehow it is you that ends up on these pages
Thumbing through every word I have written
And your name is spelled out
Letter
By
Letter
You are the muse and the music
And the stars and the sky
The way this love for you bleeds onto every line
Into everything I do
I can't get you out of my head or my poetry
But this is not the poem
You are the poem

-musings

I never quite believed in luck until the day my heart stumbled
across you
I was lucky to meet you
lucky to have you in my life every day since
lucky to witness the way the sun kisses your eyelids
and how you look at my body as if it was the only temple to ever
exist
I'm lucky to see the stars in your eyes and taste the moon on your
lips
and how I've truly never been to church until I'm citing scripture
between bite me harder thighs
wrapping my mouth around your body like black lace lingerie
and pinning your curls back with my grip so gentle
I am lucky to have tasted every curve crevice and scar
to have tied your arms around your back with roses
paralyzing you with looks and shaking you with the rolling
thunder of my touch
until I fucked the universe out of you and made wishes on your
sweet shooting stars
lucky to have a love that picks flowers for me just because
and wipes my tears away with gentle meaning
I've died a thousand times
But I finally made it to heaven
I am the luckiest girl alive
because I am alive with you

-lucky girl

Look into my eyes
Try to hold my gaze
But I break
I cave
My cheeks are hot and insecurities on fire
You grab my chin and lift it towards you
No longer looking at me
But venturing deep within
Your thumb caressing the freckles across my face
The warmth of your skin on mine makes my spine shiver
I try to look at anything but you and this time I can't look away
Our eyes meet and I can feel the blood rush all over again
Focus
Focus
I can't focus
You look at me like love and I can hardly match your stare
The sheer intensity of your attention makes me shy
But when you touch my fear so gently
You turn it into something I can conquer

-love me shy

For years I have been trapped,
Suffering,
Longing for an escape.
Buried 5 feet and 9 inches above the ground;
A walking travesty,
A ghost wrapped in flesh.
Floating through the mundane that ebbs at my heart like waves on
the shore;
Drowning in it as if every day were a tsunami,
As if I were nothing more than a stone settled at the bottom.
I never cared much for oceans until I saw the emerald sea that is
your eyes.
These waves brought you to my shore and you became the life raft
that pulled me back to the surface;
Your heart resuscitates mine as your love breathes me back to life.
I suffer no more because you are my escape,
And the ghosts of my past have finally died.

-learning to swim

When I was younger I cared nothing of love
Or finding someone to share it with
It wasn't until I had my first taste of that bittersweet drug
That I decided this is something I'd crack my knuckles and break
my wrists trying to hold onto
Something I'd be willing to fight to the death for, every single day
And since then, that's exactly what I've done
Fight
And fight
And fight
To hold onto loves that ultimately ended in nothing but little
deaths
I've come to realize that I'm a lover and a fighter
But only a fighter for love
I have always been ready to go to war for people
Who are so afraid of losing
That they never even lace up their boots

-losing the war

To the ones who loved her before me,
I have questions that need answers.
I would bet that you fell in love with her for all the same reasons I
did, and then some, because I am still learning her.
So tell me this:
How could you look into those beautiful green eyes and be the
reason tears fell from them?
How could you see such a warm and inviting smile and search for
ways to make it disappear?
What is so wrong with you that you sat and listened to the beauti-
fully earthshaking melody that is her laughter, and still took it away,
only to leave her crying hysterically for months on end?
Where did you find the audacity to freely take the heart she trusted
in your hands and throw it to the ground, watch it break, and decide it
still wasn't broken enough?
What possessed you to shatter it even more?
You didn't love her.
Maybe, at first, you thought you could.
And you pretended to love her just well enough to keep her
addicted to your games.
You smiled in her face and put knives in her back;
You kissed her cheeks and wrapped barbed wire around her heart.
You took genuine love and reduced it to only wasted time and
effort.
You broke her,
And I refuse to forgive you for it.
I refuse to forgive you for hurting a girl who only wanted to show
you she was a safe place to fall.
And god knows you made her think you were, too.

But you weren't;
You were a trap,
A ball and chain strapped to her ankles,
A set of handcuffs made entirely of thorns,
You were the devil dressed as one of the most beautiful angels she'd ever seen.
You caught her up, chained her to her past, you showed her love was a rose with no petals and put a real life angel through living hell.
And though she believes you ruined her, I disagree.
You didn't ruin anything but your only shot at real love.
You don't know a goddamn thing about love.
You didn't ruin her;
You just handed her new bricks, with all the ways you hurt her, to build the walls around her heart with.
She's guarded because of what you did to her,
She's afraid to feel,
Afraid to love,
Afraid to hurt like that again.
How do you sleep at night?
Knowing that you did this to someone so true and so good to you?
Without her,
Like you deserve.
But, I also want to take a moment to thank you.
I want to thank you for leaving a girl you knew was just too good for you.
Thank you for opening up the one place I truly belong and have been waiting my whole life to find.
Thank you for showing her what love is not,
So that when she tastes how sweet my love is,
She'll know your bitterness was never what love should've tasted like in the first place.
Thank you for the walls you helped and forced her to build,

For when I finally break them down,
The time and effort it took will show her that I mean every word
I've said to her.
My patience and relentlessness will prove that I'm here to hold her
hands, kiss her battle wounds, blow the dust off her heart, and love
her.
I'm going to love her, from her kinky mess of curls that drive me
wild,
To her size 11 feet that I want standing next to me through any and
everything.
I'm going to love her soul and her mind and her good and her bad
and her light and her dark.
Because you never knew how to.
And because you hurt her so badly,
I have been given the chance to take the most breathtaking but
broken soul,
And love all of its pieces into a mosaic more beautiful than the way
you found it.
To the one who made the biggest mistake of your life by doing his
to her,
Thank you for giving me such a blessing to hold and to cherish
forevermore.

-little treasure
12/ 26/ 16

It's been all these years
And you are still a little treasure.
Your kinky mess of curls may be gone now
But the way your hair falls still drives me wild.
Your precious heart is a little harder now
But I'm still watching it shatter in all the wrong hands.
Your battle wounds are tattooed on your skin now,
But it still looks like strength to me.
Your dark has gotten darker,
Your light has gotten brighter
And it all still just looks like love to me.
Your emerald sea fuck eyes are still worthy of drowning in.
Your laugh is still my favorite song.
Your walls have been built taller,
And stronger,
And you're still afraid to fall
Afraid to hurt
To love.
But I am still patient.
I am still waiting,
Hoping,
Holding onto the idea that you will let me in
And let me love you
The way nobody has before.
Let me love you the way I've been trying to for so long.

-little treasure

part 2

2022

Let's talk about how saving me is a constant battle and you're ready
for war
Let's talk about how you only feel at home when you're furthest
from it
Let's talk about the way my mind wanders to the memories you've
all but taken with you
Let's talk about the way you kissed me for the first time and seared
your name into my bones
Let's talk about your absence being so heavy it feels like presence
Let's talk about how we lived through so many seasons together
and now that you're gone it's always cold.
Let's talk about the way my heartbeat hesitates when your kiss
meets mine and I never prayed for a heart attack until now
Let's talk about how I never had intentions of staying in a place I'm
not welcome but loving you is home to me
Let's talk about the way my veins ache when I think about you
Let's talk about how I can't stop the world but if I could capture the
stars and turn them into constellations that resemble you,
I would
Can we talk about the way I'm willing to die for so many thing,
But I'm willing to live for you?
Can we talk?

-little talks

I exist in such a way that all I ever make is scars and bruises and
broken hearts.
For myself and for everyone around me.
I am sharp claws and shark teeth and razor blade tongues with
barbed-wire hands that feel the need to wrap around anyone who gets
too close.
They try to leave
but every move they make only tangles them up tighter,
cutting them deeper,
pulling them closer.
There is no escaping the grip I have on some people.
Some are just as doomed as I am.

-i'm sorry

It's not a fear of being alone
it's the fear of being without you
I'm not afraid of lonely
as a matter of fact I'm perfectly comfortable in my solitude
but the idea of not having you by my side that's not alone
that's not lonely
no
no that's empty
that's half a heart, half a soul
Having comfort in solitude requires peace and without you there is
no peace
I'd be waging wars between my heart and my head
but they're both fighting for you
you are the beginning and the end
you are light and dark
you are soft and scarred
You are peace
you are comfort
you are home
you are home
but I am locked out without a key
I don't have anyone to call to let me sleep on their couch until the
door is unlocked
and I can come back home
So I'll sleep on the porch
afraid of the night
because I am both lonely and alone

-homesick

I promise I mean it when I say I'm happy for you
I'm just a little lost.
Was it her on your mind when you were kissing me?
We're you pretending it was her skin touching yours that night?
I'm screaming in my dreams
And numb when I'm awake.
How do I forget you when you're everywhere I look?
How do I pretend when it's your name that's on my skin?
And I know this can't be goodbye
Because we've been here so many times before
But that doesn't mean it doesn't feel like the first time
Every time.
And I really am happy for you
But the longer I go without you
The emptier my body feels
And I'm sleeping with the lights on until you find your way back
home
Because this house is haunted when you're not here
And I'm just as hollow inside

-haunted

Smoking is a bad habit of mine
(*You are a bad habit of mine*)
But I'm not addicted to the nicotine
(*I'm addicted to you*)
It just feels nice to have something to hold onto again
(*I haven't touched a soul since you left*)
Even if it's just for five minutes
(*Feels like how long you stayed with me*)
But it is ruining my lungs
(*You took my breath away*)
It's hard to breathe
(*It's hard to breathe*)
I'm going to quit soon
(*I don't think I'll ever move on*)
So I can start breathing again
(*I can't breathe without you*)

-habits

Life has not been kind to you
Yet you still face every day ready to fight for the smile on your face
I admire your strength
Your dedication
Your commitment
To a better day than the one before
Always finding another reason to wipe away your own tears
And hold your own hand
Always fighting for the light when the world is so heavy
You deserve it all
And I will never stop going out of my way for you
Even if it's never offered in return
Because I believe in karma
And I just want to be what you deserve

-good karma

Thinking of you lately leaves me speechless
breathless most days
how many funerals have I held for you
how many little black dresses can one girl own
I'm running out of outfits to lay you to rest
and words to speak as your eulogy
I don't want to keep mourning you like this
I don't want to keep missing you like this
the ink doesn't even have time to dry anymore before I am making
arrangements again
how many tears does it take to flood the earth and bring you back
here one last time
how many empty prayers to a sky full of you does it take to bring
you back to life
I'm crying with the moon and screaming these dreams of you
and hoping to run into your ghost again
maybe in the next lifetime you'll come back as someone who can
love me

-ghost of you

I almost did it again
I almost let this love slip by me
I almost stayed
And I almost lost
I was at a crossroads
I was stuck
Do I stay in misery because it's comfortable?
Do I run as fast as my heart will let me until it pumps fresh blood?
One day it was dark
The next, all I can remember is running.
I chose to run.
Run until my blood was cleansed and free of the chains that tried to
keep me.
I am free
I am happy
I am in loving hands
Strong hands
Caring hands
S a f e hands

-almost forced away angels

I've got gardens blooming in my bones in all the same places your
hands have been.
Butterflies fluttering around to keep this love alive.
Sunshine glistens off your dewdrop eyes
And these roots grow stronger every day.
Hummingbirds stop by to drink the same sweet nectar we drink,
The honeybees want a sip too.
I don't mind sharing this garden we grew
Because what started as a seed has flourished to feed us for an
eternity,
And I want to grow with you.

-flourish

I want to ask you how your day was
I want to wish you good mornings
I want to wish you good nights
but I can't
so instead I'll wonder
and fill in the blanks myself
did you wake up ready to conquer the world this morning
did you wake up anxious
did you wake up hopeful
did you have a good day
I hope you did
did you give yourself some grace
some room to make a mistake
did something or someone make you laugh today
I hope you shared your smile with someone
I miss being that someone
did you cry
was there someone to wipe the tears away
were you longing
aching
I hope there was someone to sit beside you in the emptiness of
those heavy moments
did you think of me
because I've been thinking about you since you left
did she kiss you
did she make you feel loved today
did she make sure you know that you were wanted, needed, ap-
preciated
did she check off all the boxes today

will she tomorrow
do you miss me
are you ever coming back
do you feel like something is missing without me too
does she love the freckle above your right ear
the birthmark next to your left
did you have a good day
I hope you had a good day

-filling in the blanks

You are not just a person
You are a map of bones and veins and scars
That lead me to more places than I've ever dared venture before.
Your past is dark but your history enlightens me
As it rolls off your tequila soaked tongue.
It seems as if alcohol is the key to opening up long forgotten pieces
of people
That they tried to bury underground.
So you keep drinking
And I'll keep digging
And maybe one day I will have traveled
Every repressed map you hold inside of you.

-exploring

Come back here
Even if just for a night
Give me one more perfect night
Lay me down in your bed and slide in close to me
Drape your arm across my chest
Lay your head into the space between my shoulder and my jaw
Just the right fit.
Trace your fingers along my arms,
Let me hear you say those sweet nothings one more time.
The sweet nothings that make my heart ache just looking at my
skin
For I see the freckles you told me you loved
I feel the phantom of your touch sending chills across my body.
Just one more chance to love you the way we loved
Before fear knocked on your heart
And you let it in.

-empty

And as the morning sun wakes
It filters through the sheer curtains
Covering my body
My bed
My life
I'm a soft warm glow
And as I start to open my eyes
And rub the sleep out of them
Before I realize where I am
Before it all sets back in for another day
The memory of your love
Lays beside me in this empty space

-dreaming again

I cannot breathe I am suffocating
I keep gasping for air and I can't catch my breath
Every time I open my mouth
My lungs fill with liquid concrete
To try to fill me with something
Because since you left I have been so empty
And god dammit I feel my lungs collapsing
And I think I am too
Because I cannot seem to hold myself up anymore

-a love so heavy

Regrets collect like old friends
to relive your darkest moments.

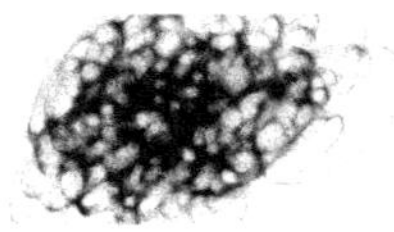

I'm not sure what I'm searching for
Or if I'm even searching
It feels more like floating
Drifting through my days
Not sure where I'm going
Or what I want
Or if there's even anything out there for me
I don't know much about this life
But I do know that every second spent without you by my side
Is another second spent aching for you

-wandering

You were here for me to lean on when I couldn't hold myself up
but even the strongest beams can't support a weight so heavy.
I cried an ocean of tears so I could drown and from the bottom I
could see you and her splashing on the surface.
I learned to use the empty spaces between breaths to fill the void
and I was doing fine until you came back to suffocate me.
You put my life to a melody and now I can't listen to the radio for
fear of forgetting how we sounded.
I search for you in crowded places but I can never find you because
you're always hidden in her shadows.
She broke your heart and you begged for mercy but she's not the
god you made her out to be and I know how you feel.
She is to you what you are to me and you run to me for help but
you can't find me in the chaos you left behind.
I am buried beneath broken memories and shattered pieces of
myself and you've never been the kind to dig.
You were never the kind to dig until she used her claws to rip the
ground out from under us and handed you a shovel to finish what she
started.
Adele and I both know I must've called a thousand times but you
can't hear anything other than her broken record voice.
You and I have both moved on from our past but I still torture
myself with occasional visits that last far too long.
You look right past me but I know you and I know me and that's
why my heart sinks every time you pretend I'm not there.
If I could turn back time I'd turn these disconnections into
reconnections and show you just what you were going to do to me.
Your regrets are blinded by her light and I wear mine on my body
like battle wounds from fighting the urge to need you.

I have spent so much of my time loving you in secret
But you have never been a secret.
You have never been a question
But always the answer.
Do you think maybe we lived in a past life?
With all the maybes that exist
I hope that maybe we end up together in another life.
I often wonder if we ever think of each other at the same time
The passion in our kiss
The electricity in our embrace
The unspoken that remains that way and is still understood
The way you take up every little space inside of me
And yet I still crave you
The way we are so vulnerable together
But somehow just keep missing each other
But there is no rush
I would be happy to spend forever loving and learning you
I would spend lifetimes waiting
If that's what it took to hold your heart again
If I could love you in every eternity
It still would not be enough

-desire

Today I discovered an all new set of dusks. I suffered months without a single sunset and if you know anything about me you're probably questioning my sanity and I question my own sanity now that hindsight's 20/20. What the hell was I thinking? Why was I trying so hard to be the water to put out the flames and turn a living hell into a pseudo heaven? All I know is that I was the spark that set your gasoline hands on fire and ignited everything around me until it was ash and all I know is that I walked through Hell's flames and maybe I got burned but god dammit I survived. We had it all once upon a time but if the light goes out was it ever really there? You had me fooled for a pretty little while until a strong wind of self love blew away all your smoke and cracked all the mirrors your fists left untouched. It's true what they say, love is blind or maybe blinding or maybe I was blinded by my own expectations and dreams we could never live up to. Butterflies in my stomach turned into knots once I realized you weren't who you pretended to be. I had fingernails. I had fingernails before your love turned into doors locking me out and a heart that did too. The sound of those doors slamming shut in my face haunts me on random street corners some days. Most days. I really am doing better though. I don't cry for you, because of you. I don't swallow lethal cocktails anymore I don't release your demons through my wrists anymore and the blood has dried up. I'm a bird my darlings I've always been a bird and you tried to cage me you tried god dammit you tried to tame a wild wind a free spirit a flowing entity and before I knew it I was purple in the face and begging for a chance to catch my breath. Rock bottom has a basement, I know, I found it. I tried to make a home out of it and when I say basement I'm not talking a broken light bulb and dust covered clutter, no. No. I'm talking about a basement that feels like an ocean with no bottom, endless cold and darkness and you're descending faster than your brain can comprehend and you try to flail your way to the surface only to realize you've got anchors tied to your feet only sinking deeper as time passes. I'm talking about the kind of basement your worst nightmares and biggest fears are afraid to lurk in. And you're trying so goddamn hard not to gasp for air or scream or open your mouth because you're drowning remember you're already under water and you can't tell which way is up anymore my dear do you know that kind of darkness? My dear, do you think a certain shade of dark can trick you into seeing stars when there are none, until you learn to love your own light? Do you think drowning sometimes cleanses you from the inside out, killing only the parts of you that hold you under so that you can finally break the surface?

-D Day

Darkness and I know each other on a first name basis.
We've spent countless nights tangled up in bed sheets together.
Darkness has a grip that feels like death and I just needed something to hold me while you were gone.
Little did I know Darkness would sink its claws all the way into my bones, sharpening them with my insides, and cut my veins open to drain you from everything that I once was.
Darkness clings to my side, carries marionette strings in its pocket just in case I try to escape the hold it has on me.
I clean my glasses every morning but I still see nothing but black by mid-afternoon.
Cloudy doesn't even begin to explain the way I've been seeing things since Darkness and I became one.
I look and I see nothing. I see empty. Hollow and too vast for any form of comfort.
Darkness has taken my hands and tied them together and led me by rope, blindfolded, into a void I never imagined existed.
They say your other senses become stronger when one is taken away. That's not true at all.
Darkness took away my sight, and when it binded my hands, took my grip on reality.
I try to listen for other voices but I hear nothing.
Like there's mud packed into my ear cavities and I'm so deep under the surface of river water that all I can feel is the pressure popping in my ears. I can't taste anything but the muddy grit between my teeth from trying to scream under water.
Darkness won't let go of me no matter how much I beg and plead and I know now there is only one way out.
-darkness

Sometimes you say their name
And it sounds like a confession.
A secret you've been afraid to share for so long.
You carry this confession deep within,
You always choose date so you don't slip up.
Hiding hard blows and harder truths in the darkest shadows.
Pretending you don't feel the poison coursing with each beat of the
heart.
Pretending it doesn't hurt anymore
Pretending it doesn't burn the same way the alcohol does each time
you try to drown them out.
You tell half truths and puzzle pieces to avoid the demons but all
you're doing is feeding them in the dark.
Sometimes you say their name and it sounds like a confession.
So confess.
Confess.
Confess.

-confessions in the dark

Finding hope and meaning in this life has never been a skill of
mine.
I have seen mornings with no sunrise
Days with no light
Nights with not a star in the sky.
Yet here I stand
Once again
Lungs still breathing
Heart still beating to the same empty rhythm it's been dancing to
like a puppet for as long as I can remember.
I rise every morning
Just to fall again at dusk.
I have nothing to keep me holding on
But somehow my knuckles are still white and cracking
From the force expended to grasp my every day life.
I may be a lone midnight with tunnel vision now
but I will not be blind forever.
One day my eyelids will begin to separate
And the darkness will begin to dissipate
And my grip will loosen
And the rain will be warm again
And light will seep into every crack and crevice of my hopeless but
so hopeful little soul.

-calm after the storm

Yes I know it's over and yes I know nothing I could do in a thousand years would ever change it but holy fuck I'm not over it I'm not I have to have closure from everything that has led me to open wounds and I just cannot seem to find it I have been searching for some kind of bandage for all this bleeding that everyone swore would be temporary because according to them "time heals all wounds" but I am still fucking bleeding and maybe I haven't given these wounds enough time to heal but if I don't see a scab or scar forming soon I swear I am going to drown in my own blood and still have to take the blame for fucking up everything because instead of opening my mouth to say something I try so hard to open my fucking veins

-leaving bones exposed

I promised to always leave a light on for you if you ever left.
I buy a new candle every day.
Bathroom floors have become more welcoming since you walked
out the door.
But it is never locked.
And I have this feeling that the end of the world is going to look a
lot like my heart does without you.
I'm filling these pages with all the right words at all the wrong
times
To remind myself that I'll never be enough for you.
And that's me you hear slipping barefoot through your dreams,
And I'm running out of pretty words and poetry,
Just the constant and lingering thought of you.
Sometimes I sit alone in silence
And I can still hear the noise.
I am trying to unlearn everything about you
But I don't think I'll ever know how to let go with grace.
And this is not poetry anymore,
This is me begging you to come back through the tip of a pen
Dry heaving the ache
Trying to catch my breath each time I'm reminded
Each time I look at my skin.
The freckles, the ink, the places you've been
It all hurts.
But I'll keep you buried deep
And allow the ache to rot my core
Until next spring when you're in full bloom again
And maybe next season
I'll hold a steadier hand,

I won't overwater it
And drown out everything I've sown.
I hope to bloom from where I once bled,
And I want growth from all of this dead.
-bloom from where I once bled

In this life I have learned one thing that proves to hold true:
It happens,
The good, and the bad, all of it happens to all of us.
And then it leaves you with two choices.
You either get better,
Or you get bitter.
You take it as it comes, and make the most of what you have left
after it goes;
Or you fight it,
You go to war with every card you're dealt,
And you let it destroy you.
I have always been one to strap on my armor and fight some things
to the death.
And it has only left me more broken, beaten, and bruised.
I am slowly teaching myself to let life happen as it comes,
And make the most of what's left,
Instead of only mourning all that was lost.
I want better,
I am so goddamn tired of being bitter.

I'd like to think I'd be better off if I never met you
but I'm finding it hard to convince myself
maybe I'd be living a completely different life right now had I never
stumbled into your path
Then I wonder what kind of life is worth not knowing you
and I draw a blank
I can't imagine a single day I've been a part of
somehow being better without the thought of you visiting at least
once
I can't imagine looking at the sun and not feeling the heat of your
touch
I can't fathom looking at the wildflowers outside my window
and not seeing your smile blooming alongside them
Trying not to hear your voice
your laugh
in the wind
the bird song
on every radio station
I don't know how to watch the sunlight reflect off the creek behind
my home
and not see the glint in your eyes
I don't know how not to find pieces of you
in every single day
I'd like to think I'd be better off if I never met you
but even my worst days are easier
because I know you

-better off

You showed up at an old friend's funeral
and I couldn't help but wonder if you'd have the audacity to show
your face at mine.
Would you still be in disbelief even though you saw this coming
the first time you saved me from it?
Would you put on a show and tell everyone how close we used to
be?
Will you tell them the story of the time I loved you and you loved
me back?
And will you leave out all the parts about you leaving and breaking
my heart?
Will you forget to mention that I begged for your love only to have
you act like I was a stranger when we ran into each other?
Will you tell them about how you said you couldn't stand the
thought of losing me the first night I tried to die,
then left me the very next morning?
I bet you forget to remember all the hell you put me through so
nobody questions if these are your initials carved into my casket.
Tell them how I clawed at your bones to try to keep you here and
all you did was twist out of my grip and run.
Make it known to everyone that you ruined the only one who ever
truly cared for you and now she's dead and gone and you can't
apologize.
And I hope you're up late tossing and turning because you can't get
me out of your head and you finally understand what it was like to be
me.
I hope you have sleepless nights spent begging god to bring me
back to you, crying and drowning in hopelessness because you were
too late.

I hope you get the news about my suicide when you're having a good time and can't find a bathroom quick enough to purge your regrets.
I hope your hands shake and your eyes stay bloodshot for weeks from the restlessness and memories you can remember perfectly all of a sudden.
I hope my death distracts you from reality so badly that your mother calls you every night to make sure you're still eating enough.
I hope you see how much you've hurt me in the purple scars on my wrists and bags under my eyes that the makeup couldn't hide at the mortuary.
I hope you lose your mind in the middle of a crowded street and fall to your knees asking god for mercy and to let you see me alive one last time.
Oh but you'll be too late.
And you'll regret wasting all the chances I gave that you never deserved.
I hope it eats you alive.
And I'll sit back and watch you go insane
from a place where it doesn't hurt to love you anymore.
-untitled 2014

Part of me will always wonder what if
But the other part of me is okay with accepting what is.
Because I know that at one point
We shared a world together
And I can always visit that world in my mind when my heart starts
searching for you again.
The memories are always as warm as the moments were,
And I'd be okay with crawling inside one
And dying there.

-all that remains

The tender warmth you left behind still haunts my skin
The laugh you left behind still echoes in all our favorite songs
The thought of you touching my skin reignites every flame
Holding a funeral for you with each memory only kills me
You visit me in my dreams and I don't want to wake up
So that I don't have to mourn you ever again
But drinking doesn't drown butterflies
And bloodletting doesn't stop the ache coursing through my veins
Every part of me that you have touched is haunted by a love so soft
They say addiction is treatable
But they've never loved a drug like you.

-addict

I don't pity you.
Pity is insulting.
Please know that when I say my heart breaks for you
it's because I know that same pain all too well.
I see that dead inside look in your eyes
and recognize it like my reflection in a mirror.
I hear the screaming in your silence.
I feel how heavy the empty is in my chest even though it isn't my
ache to carry.
I know you feel like you haven't held it long enough
but it weighs so much
and you already have the rest of the world resting on your shoul-
ders.
I'd like to hold some of it for you.
I will sit beside you in the dark
offering a safe place to lay it all down for a moment of honesty.
Take your armor off and bleed where you need to.
I'm not afraid of the dark
and a mess is not an inconvenience.
Your heavy heart is not a burden here.
This is a safe place to shatter.

-savior complex

Writing is my most honest act of living and I am so excited to finally be sharing this piece of my world with you.
This is my very first poetry book, or any book, for that matter.
I've been writing poetry for almost 10 years now and I hope that this is something I can do forever.
My teenage years showed me very little mercy, and that's where my love of writing was born.
Consider this my diary, but made palatable for readers.
This collection of poems offers a variety of feelings, from first loves, to forever loves, to teenage angst and the depths of depression.
I hope that this book, and any that come after, reaches the intended audience and makes them feel slightly less alone in this great big world.
From the bottom of my heart, thank you so much for taking time and interest in my work.
Here's to being incredibly vulnerable so that someone else feels seen, heard, understood.

www.ingramcontent.com/pod-product-compliance
Lightning Source LLC
Chambersburg PA
CBHW070918160726
48004CB00003B/1424